Enterprise Generative AI: Insights and Applications

Contents

Part I: Introduction to Generative AI

Introduction to Generative AI

What is Generative AI?

Generative AI refers to a class of artificial intelligence algorithms that generate new content, such as images, text, music, and even entire virtual worlds, from existing data. Unlike traditional AI, which focuses on recognizing patterns and making predictions, generative AI creates something new by learning from the underlying patterns in the input data. The primary goal is to mimic the creative process of humans, enabling machines to produce original, high-quality outputs.

History and Evolution of Generative AI

The concept of generative AI has been around for decades, but significant advancements have been made in recent years. Early attempts in the 1950s and 1960s focused on rule-based systems and simple probabilistic models. The development of neural networks in the 1980s and 1990s laid the foundation for modern generative models. The introduction of Generative Adversarial Networks (GANs) by Ian Goodfellow in 2014 marked a significant breakthrough, enabling the generation of highly realistic images. Since then, advancements in deep learning and computational power have accelerated the evolution of generative AI, leading to the development of sophisticated models like Variational Autoencoders (VAEs) and Transformers.

Key Concepts and Terminologies

- **Generative Model**: A model that learns to generate new data instances that resemble the training data.
- **Latent Space**: A compressed representation of the input data, capturing the underlying patterns and features.
- **Adversarial Training**: A training process where two models (generator and discriminator) compete against each other to improve the quality of generated outputs.
- **Autoencoder**: A neural network used to learn efficient representations of data by compressing and decompressing it.
- **Transformer**: A type of neural network architecture particularly effective for natural language processing tasks.

Generative AI Models and Techniques

Overview of Different Generative Models

Generative AI encompasses various models, each with unique mechanisms for generating data. The most prominent types include:

- **Generative Adversarial Networks (GANs)**: Consisting of a generator and a discriminator, GANs create data by pitting these two networks against each other.
- **Variational Autoencoders (VAEs)**: These models learn to encode data into a latent space and decode it back to the original form, with the ability to sample new data points from the latent space.
- **Transformers**: Initially designed for natural language processing, transformers generate text and other sequential data by predicting the next element in a sequence.

Generative Adversarial Networks (GANs)

GANs are composed of two neural networks: a generator and a discriminator. The generator creates new data instances, while the discriminator evaluates their authenticity. Through iterative training, the generator improves its ability to produce realistic data, while the discriminator enhances its skill in distinguishing real data from fake. This adversarial process results in highly accurate generative models capable of producing lifelike images, videos, and more.

Variational Autoencoders (VAEs)

VAEs are a type of autoencoder designed for generative tasks. They consist of an encoder, which compresses input data into a latent space, and a decoder, which reconstructs the data from this compressed representation. By incorporating probabilistic elements, VAEs can generate new data by sampling from the latent space. This makes them particularly useful for tasks requiring the generation of diverse outputs, such as image synthesis and data augmentation.

Transformers and GPT

Transformers are a neural network architecture that excels in handling sequential data, such as text. The architecture relies on self-attention mechanisms to capture relationships between different elements in a sequence. Generative Pre-trained Transformers (GPT), developed by OpenAI, are a series of transformer-based models pre-trained on vast amounts of text data. GPT models can generate coherent and contextually relevant text, making them powerful tools for applications like text completion, translation, and conversation generation.

Applications of Generative AI

Use Cases in Various Industries

Generative AI has a wide range of applications across different industries:

- **Healthcare**: Drug discovery, medical imaging, and personalized treatment plans.
- **Entertainment**: Content creation, video game design, and virtual reality.
- **Finance**: Fraud detection, algorithmic trading, and risk assessment.
- **Retail**: Product design, recommendation systems, and inventory management.
- **Automotive**: Autonomous vehicle design, traffic simulation, and predictive maintenance.

Benefits and Challenges

The benefits of generative AI include:

- **Creativity and Innovation**: Enabling the creation of novel content and solutions.

- **Efficiency**: Automating complex tasks and reducing human effort.

- **Personalization**: Tailoring products and services to individual preferences.

However, there are also challenges:

- **Quality Control**: Ensuring the generated outputs meet quality standards.

- **Ethical Concerns**: Addressing issues like data privacy, bias, and misuse of AI.

- **Technical Complexity**: Developing and maintaining advanced generative models requires significant expertise and resources.

Case Studies

1. **Healthcare**: Generative AI models have been used to generate synthetic medical images, aiding in the development of diagnostic tools and reducing the need for large labeled datasets.

2. **Entertainment**: In the gaming industry, AI has been used to create realistic character animations and expansive virtual worlds, enhancing the gaming experience.

3. **Finance**: Generative models have been employed to simulate market conditions, helping financial institutions in stress testing and risk management.

Part II: Implementing Generative AI in Enterprises

Setting Up the Foundation

Building a Data Strategy

A successful generative AI implementation begins with a robust data strategy. Data is the lifeblood of AI, and a well-defined strategy ensures that data is collected, managed, and utilized effectively.

1. **Data Collection**: Identify the types of data needed and establish processes for gathering this data from various sources, including internal databases, customer interactions, and third-party datasets.

2. **Data Quality**: Ensure the data is accurate, complete, and free from biases. Implement data cleaning and preprocessing steps to enhance data quality.

3. **Data Governance**: Develop policies for data management, including data ownership, privacy, and security. This ensures compliance with legal and regulatory requirements and protects sensitive information.

4. **Data Storage**: Choose appropriate storage solutions that can handle large volumes of data and provide easy access for AI models. Consider cloud-based storage for scalability and flexibility.

5. **Data Accessibility**: Make data accessible to the teams that need it while maintaining security. Use data cataloging and management tools to organize and streamline access.

Infrastructure and Tools

The right infrastructure and tools are critical for supporting generative AI projects. This includes both hardware and software components.

1. **Computing Power**: Generative AI models, especially deep learning models, require substantial computational resources. Invest in powerful GPUs or TPUs, and consider cloud-based solutions for scalability.

2. **Software Frameworks**: Utilize popular AI frameworks such as TensorFlow, PyTorch, and Keras. These frameworks provide pre-built models and tools for developing, training, and deploying generative AI models.

3. **Data Pipelines**: Implement robust data pipelines to automate the process of data ingestion, preprocessing, model training, and deployment. Tools like Apache Airflow and Kubeflow can help manage these workflows.

4. **Collaboration Tools**: Facilitate collaboration among team members with tools like Jupyter notebooks, Git for version control, and project management platforms.

Talent and Skill Requirements

Building a generative AI team requires a mix of skills and expertise. The following roles are essential:

1. **Data Scientists**: Experts in statistics, machine learning, and data analysis who develop and fine-tune generative AI models.

2. **Data Engineers**: Professionals who design and maintain the data infrastructure, ensuring data is available and accessible for AI projects.

3. **AI Researchers**: Specialists who stay abreast of the latest advancements in AI and explore new algorithms and techniques.

4. **Software Engineers**: Developers who integrate AI models into applications, ensuring they work seamlessly within the existing IT ecosystem.

5. **Domain Experts**: Individuals with deep knowledge of the specific industry or business domain, providing valuable insights and ensuring AI solutions address real-world problems.

Chapter : Transforming Business Models with Generative AI

In recent years, the advent of Generative AI has fundamentally altered the landscape of business models across industries. Companies are no longer limited to traditional methods of production and service delivery; instead, they are leveraging advanced algorithms to create new products, streamline operations, and enhance customer experiences. The implications of this technology are profound, offering unprecedented opportunities for innovation and growth.

Generative AI, particularly through models like GPT-4, enables businesses to generate high-quality content, automate complex processes, and provide personalized services at scale. This chapter delves into the transformative potential of Generative AI, exploring its applications across various sectors, including marketing, finance, and supply chain management.

Reimagining Product Development

At the heart of Generative AI's impact is its ability to revolutionize product development. Companies are increasingly utilizing AI-driven design tools to prototype and iterate products rapidly. For instance, in the fashion industry, brands are employing Generative AI to create unique clothing designs based on current trends and consumer preferences. By analyzing vast datasets of past designs, customer feedback, and social media trends, AI can suggest innovative styles that resonate with target audiences.

In the automotive sector, manufacturers are using AI to simulate vehicle designs, testing their aerodynamics and safety features in virtual environments. This not only accelerates the design process but also reduces the costs associated with physical prototyping. Generative AI allows engineers to explore a broader range of design possibilities, leading to more efficient and sustainable vehicles.

Enhancing Marketing Strategies

Marketing strategies are also being transformed through the use of Generative AI. Personalized marketing has emerged as a critical component of successful campaigns, and AI can tailor content to individual consumer preferences. Through natural language processing (NLP), Generative AI can analyze customer interactions, purchase histories, and social media behaviors to create highly targeted marketing messages.

For example, AI-driven platforms can generate email campaigns that adapt to each recipient's interests, increasing engagement rates and driving conversions. Additionally, generative models can create dynamic ad content that evolves based on real-time performance metrics. This agility in marketing not only enhances customer experiences but also maximizes return on investment (ROI) for advertising budgets.

Automating Customer Service

Another significant application of Generative AI lies in automating customer service operations. AI-powered chatbots and virtual assistants can handle a wide range of customer inquiries, providing instant support without the need for human intervention. These systems utilize generative models to understand context and generate coherent, relevant responses, enhancing user satisfaction.

Companies such as Zendesk and Drift are pioneering the integration of AI into customer service frameworks, allowing businesses to maintain high service levels while reducing operational costs. By handling routine inquiries, AI enables human agents to focus on more complex issues, ultimately improving service efficiency and customer loyalty.

Streamlining Supply Chain Management

Generative AI's capabilities extend to supply chain management, where it can optimize logistics, inventory management, and demand forecasting. Advanced algorithms analyze historical data, market trends, and external factors to generate insights that drive strategic decision-making.

For instance, AI can predict fluctuations in demand based on seasonal trends and consumer behavior, allowing businesses to adjust inventory levels proactively. Additionally, AI-driven simulations can identify the most efficient shipping routes, minimizing costs and delivery times. This level of optimization leads to a more agile and responsive supply chain, critical in today's fast-paced market.

Redefining Financial Services

In the financial sector, Generative AI is redefining how institutions operate, offering new approaches to risk assessment, fraud detection, and personalized financial planning. By analyzing vast datasets, AI models can identify patterns and anomalies that may indicate fraudulent activities, enabling faster and more accurate responses to potential threats.

Furthermore, AI-driven robo-advisors are transforming personal finance management. These platforms leverage Generative AI to create personalized investment strategies based on individual risk profiles, financial goals, and market conditions. This democratization of financial advice allows consumers access to sophisticated investment strategies that were previously available only to wealthier individuals.

Conclusion

The applications of Generative AI across various industries illustrate its transformative potential. As businesses embrace this technology, they are reimagining their operations, enhancing customer experiences, and driving innovation. The future of enterprise is increasingly intertwined with AI, leading to new business models that prioritize agility, personalization, and efficiency. In the following chapters, we will explore specific case studies and strategies for implementing Generative AI effectively within organizations, ensuring sustained competitive advantage in an evolving marketplace.

Chapter : Ethical Considerations in Generative AI Deployment

As Generative AI continues to proliferate across industries, it is imperative for organizations to address the ethical considerations associated with its deployment. The power of AI to create content, influence decisions, and automate processes raises important questions about accountability, bias, and transparency. This chapter explores the ethical challenges posed by Generative AI and outlines best practices for responsible implementation.

Understanding Bias in AI Models

One of the most pressing ethical concerns in Generative AI is the potential for bias in AI models. Bias can emerge from various sources, including the datasets used to train models, the algorithms employed, and the cultural contexts in which AI operates. If not addressed, bias can lead to unfair outcomes, reinforcing stereotypes and discrimination.

For example, an AI model trained on historical hiring data may inadvertently learn and perpetuate biases present in that data. If the training dataset reflects a lack of diversity, the resulting AI system may favor certain demographic groups over others, leading to discriminatory hiring practices.

Organizations must adopt a proactive approach to identify and mitigate bias in their AI models. This includes conducting thorough audits of training datasets, employing techniques for bias detection and correction, and ensuring diverse representation among the teams developing AI solutions.

Ensuring Transparency and Accountability

Transparency is another critical aspect of ethical AI deployment. Stakeholders, including customers, employees, and regulators, should understand how AI systems operate and make decisions. This is particularly important in applications that impact individuals' lives, such as healthcare, finance, and law enforcement.

To promote transparency, organizations should provide clear explanations of AI decision-making processes. Techniques such as explainable AI (XAI) can help demystify complex models, enabling users to understand how outcomes are generated. For instance, in a healthcare setting, AI systems used for diagnosis should clearly communicate the factors influencing their recommendations, allowing medical professionals to make informed decisions.

Accountability is equally important in the ethical use of Generative AI. Organizations must establish clear lines of responsibility for AI outcomes, ensuring that there are mechanisms in place to address any negative consequences that may arise from AI deployment. This includes implementing governance frameworks that define roles, responsibilities, and oversight for AI systems.

The Role of Human Oversight

Despite the capabilities of Generative AI, human oversight remains essential. Organizations should not rely solely on AI to make critical decisions, particularly in high-stakes environments. Instead, AI should be viewed as a tool that augments human judgment rather than replaces it.

In the context of customer service, for example, AI chatbots can handle routine inquiries, but human agents should be available to address complex issues. This hybrid approach ensures that AI serves to enhance the overall customer experience while maintaining the human touch that is often necessary for nuanced interactions.

Additionally, organizations should establish protocols for human review of AI-generated content. This is particularly important in creative fields, where the potential for generating inappropriate or harmful content exists. By incorporating human oversight, organizations can maintain quality and ethical standards in their AI outputs.

Addressing Environmental Sustainability

The deployment of Generative AI also raises environmental concerns, particularly regarding energy consumption and resource usage. Training large AI models requires substantial computational power, often leading to a significant carbon footprint. As organizations adopt AI technologies, it is crucial to consider their environmental impact and seek sustainable practices.

Companies can mitigate their environmental impact by investing in energy-efficient infrastructure, utilizing cloud services that prioritize sustainability, and exploring ways to optimize model training processes. Additionally, organizations should assess the lifecycle impact of their AI solutions, considering factors such as resource extraction, energy usage, and end-of-life disposal.

Conclusion

As Generative AI continues to shape industries, ethical considerations must remain at the forefront of deployment strategies. By addressing bias, ensuring transparency, maintaining human oversight, and prioritizing sustainability, organizations can navigate the ethical landscape of AI responsibly. The following chapters will focus on governance frameworks, risk management strategies, and practical approaches for integrating ethical principles into the development and deployment of Generative AI solutions.

Chapter : Governance Frameworks for Generative AI

As organizations increasingly adopt Generative AI technologies, establishing robust governance frameworks becomes essential. These frameworks provide the necessary structures, policies, and processes to ensure responsible AI deployment, aligning with ethical standards and regulatory requirements. This chapter explores the key components of effective governance frameworks for Generative AI and offers practical guidance for organizations seeking to implement them.

Defining Governance Structures

A critical first step in developing a governance framework is defining the organizational structure responsible for AI oversight. This involves appointing dedicated teams or committees tasked with AI governance, including stakeholders from various functions such as data science, legal, compliance, and ethics. These teams should collaborate to establish clear roles and responsibilities, ensuring that AI initiatives align with the organization's strategic objectives and ethical principles.

Additionally, organizations should consider forming an AI ethics board composed of diverse experts who can provide guidance on ethical implications and potential risks associated with AI deployment. This board can play a crucial role in evaluating AI projects, offering recommendations, and promoting a culture of accountability within the organization.

Establishing Policies and Guidelines

Effective governance frameworks should include comprehensive policies and guidelines that address key aspects of AI deployment. This includes data governance policies that outline data collection, usage, storage, and sharing practices. Organizations must ensure that they adhere to legal and regulatory requirements regarding data privacy and protection, particularly when handling sensitive information.

Furthermore, policies should address model development practices, emphasizing the importance of bias detection and mitigation strategies. Organizations should establish protocols for auditing AI models regularly, assessing their performance and ensuring that they remain fair and unbiased over time.

In addition to internal policies, organizations should stay informed about evolving regulations and standards related to AI. Engaging with industry associations and regulatory bodies can provide valuable insights into best practices and emerging guidelines, helping organizations remain compliant while navigating the complex AI landscape.

Implementing Risk Management Strategies

Risk management is a vital component of AI governance, as it enables organizations to identify, assess, and mitigate potential risks associated with AI deployment. This includes operational risks, reputational risks, and compliance risks that may arise from AI use.

Organizations should conduct comprehensive risk assessments for AI initiatives, evaluating factors such as data quality, model accuracy, and potential biases. This assessment should consider the broader implications of AI deployment, including impacts on stakeholders and societal norms.

To manage risks effectively, organizations can implement monitoring and evaluation processes that track AI performance over time. Regular audits of AI systems can help identify deviations from expected behavior, allowing organizations to address issues proactively before they escalate into significant problems.

Promoting a Culture of Accountability

Cultivating a culture of accountability is essential for ensuring that AI governance frameworks are effective. Organizations should foster an environment where employees feel empowered to raise concerns about AI initiatives and report any unethical practices. This includes implementing whistleblower protections and providing training on ethical considerations related to AI.

Leadership commitment is crucial in promoting accountability. Executives should actively endorse AI governance initiatives, reinforcing the importance of ethical AI practices across the organization. By setting a strong tone from the top, organizations can instill a sense of responsibility among employees and encourage adherence to governance frameworks.

Engaging Stakeholders and Building Trust

Effective governance frameworks should prioritize stakeholder engagement to build trust and transparency around AI initiatives. Organizations should communicate openly with customers, employees, and other stakeholders about their AI practices, addressing concerns and providing clarity on how AI technologies are being used.

This engagement can take various forms, including public disclosures, community consultations, and stakeholder feedback mechanisms. By actively involving stakeholders in discussions about AI deployment, organizations can enhance their credibility and foster a collaborative approach to responsible AI use.

Conclusion

Establishing robust governance frameworks is essential for organizations seeking to implement Generative AI responsibly. By defining governance structures, establishing policies, implementing risk management strategies, promoting accountability, and engaging stakeholders, organizations can navigate the complexities of AI deployment effectively. As we move forward, the next chapter will explore practical strategies for integrating Generative AI into existing business processes, ensuring that organizations can leverage its capabilities while adhering to ethical and governance standards.

Chapter : Practical Strategies for Integrating Generative AI into Business Processes

The successful integration of Generative AI into existing business processes requires a strategic approach that aligns AI capabilities with organizational goals. This chapter outlines practical strategies for implementing Generative AI across various functions, ensuring that organizations can harness its potential effectively and sustainably.

Identifying Use Cases and Opportunities

The first step in integrating Generative AI is identifying specific use cases that align with business objectives. Organizations should conduct a thorough analysis of their operations, exploring areas where AI can add value, enhance efficiency, or improve customer experiences.

Common use cases for Generative AI include content generation, product design, customer service automation, and data analysis. For example, marketing teams can leverage AI to create personalized content for campaigns, while product development teams can use AI to prototype new designs rapidly. By focusing on high-impact areas, organizations can maximize the return on their AI investments.

Building Cross-Functional Teams

Successful AI integration often requires collaboration across different departments. Organizations should establish cross-functional teams that bring together experts from various domains, including data science, IT, marketing, and operations. These teams can work collaboratively to develop and implement AI solutions that meet the needs of the entire organization.

Cross-functional teams also facilitate knowledge sharing and innovation, allowing organizations to leverage diverse perspectives and expertise. This collaborative approach can lead to more effective AI solutions that address real business challenges while fostering a culture of experimentation and learning.

Investing in Training and Education

To fully realize the potential of Generative AI, organizations must invest in training and education for their employees. This includes providing resources and support for upskilling staff in AI technologies, data analysis, and ethical considerations. By empowering employees with the knowledge and skills necessary to work with AI, organizations can enhance their capabilities and foster a culture of continuous learning.

Training programs should be tailored to the specific needs of different teams, ensuring that employees understand how AI can enhance their roles. For example, marketing professionals may require training in AI-driven analytics tools, while product designers may benefit from workshops on generative design techniques.

Implementing Agile Methodologies

Integrating Generative AI into business processes is an iterative process that benefits from agility and flexibility. Organizations should adopt agile methodologies that allow for rapid experimentation, feedback, and iteration. This approach enables teams to test AI solutions quickly, gather insights, and make adjustments based on real-world performance.

Agile practices encourage collaboration and communication among teams, fostering an environment where innovation can thrive. By prioritizing experimentation and learning, organizations can continuously refine their AI solutions and adapt to changing business needs.

Ensuring Robust Data Management

Effective data management is critical for the successful integration of Generative AI. Organizations must establish processes for data collection, storage, and analysis to ensure that AI systems have access to high-quality data. This includes implementing data governance practices that prioritize data privacy, security, and compliance.

Moreover, organizations should invest in infrastructure that supports scalable data management solutions. This may involve utilizing cloud services, data lakes, or data warehouses to centralize data storage and facilitate seamless access for AI applications.

Measuring Success and Impact

To gauge the effectiveness of Generative AI integration, organizations should establish key performance indicators (KPIs) that align with their business objectives. These KPIs should encompass both quantitative and qualitative measures, assessing the impact of AI solutions on business processes, customer satisfaction, and operational efficiency.

Regular monitoring and evaluation of AI initiatives are essential for identifying areas for improvement and ensuring that projects remain aligned with organizational goals. Organizations should conduct periodic reviews to assess the performance of AI solutions, gather feedback from stakeholders, and make necessary adjustments.

Conclusion

Integrating Generative AI into business processes requires a strategic and collaborative approach that prioritizes alignment with organizational goals. By identifying use cases, building cross-functional teams, investing in training, implementing agile methodologies, ensuring robust data management, and measuring success, organizations can harness the transformative potential of AI responsibly. The next chapter will delve into future trends and innovations in Generative AI, exploring how organizations can prepare for the evolving landscape of AI technologies.

Integrating Generative AI with Business Processes

Identifying Business Opportunities

To maximize the impact of generative AI, it's essential to identify where it can add the most value within your organization.

1. **Analyze Business Needs**: Conduct a thorough analysis of your business processes to identify pain points and areas where AI can provide significant improvements.

2. **Engage Stakeholders**: Involve key stakeholders from different departments to understand their challenges and gather ideas on potential AI applications.

3. **Evaluate Feasibility**: Assess the technical feasibility and potential ROI of different AI use cases. Prioritize projects that align with strategic goals and offer clear benefits.

Aligning AI Strategies with Business Goals

Ensuring that your AI initiatives align with your overall business strategy is crucial for success.

1. **Set Clear Objectives**: Define clear, measurable objectives for your AI projects that support your business goals, whether it's improving customer satisfaction, reducing costs, or enhancing product quality.

2. **Develop a Roadmap**: Create a detailed roadmap outlining the steps needed to achieve these objectives. Include milestones, timelines, and resource allocation.

3. **Monitor Progress**: Continuously monitor the progress of AI projects and adjust the strategy as needed. Use key performance indicators (KPIs) to measure success and make data-driven decisions.

Workflow Integration

Integrating generative AI into your existing workflows requires careful planning and execution.

1. **Assess Current Workflows**: Map out your current workflows to identify where AI can be integrated. Look for tasks that can be automated or enhanced with AI-generated outputs.

2. **Design AI-Enhanced Workflows**: Redesign workflows to incorporate AI models, ensuring they complement and enhance human tasks rather than replace them. Focus on seamless integration to minimize disruption.

3. **Pilot Projects**: Start with pilot projects to test the integration of AI into specific workflows. Use these pilots to identify potential issues and refine your approach.

4. **Training and Change Management**: Provide training for employees to help them understand and work with AI-enhanced processes. Implement change management strategies to ensure smooth adoption and minimize resistance.

5. **Scale Up**: Once pilot projects are successful, scale up the integration to other parts of the organization. Continuously monitor and optimize AI-enhanced workflows to ensure they deliver the desired outcomes.

Developing Generative AI Models

Data Collection and Preprocessing

Data Collection

The success of generative AI models heavily depends on the quality and quantity of data. Proper data collection is the first critical step:

1. **Identify Data Sources**: Determine the sources of data relevant to your generative AI goals. These can include internal databases, public datasets, APIs, and user-generated content.

2. **Data Diversity**: Ensure the data encompasses a wide range of variations to improve the model's ability to generalize. This could mean collecting data across different times, locations, and contexts.

3. **Volume of Data**: Collect a sufficient volume of data to train robust models. Generative models, especially deep learning ones, often require large datasets to perform well.

4. **Data Privacy and Compliance**: Adhere to data privacy regulations such as GDPR or CCPA. Ensure you have the necessary permissions to use the data, and anonymize it if needed.

Data Preprocessing

Once data is collected, preprocessing ensures that it is in the right form for training generative models:

1. **Data Cleaning**: Remove any irrelevant or corrupted data. Handle missing values and correct inconsistencies.

2. **Normalization and Scaling**: Normalize or scale the data to ensure that it fits within a specific range. This is particularly important for numerical data.

3. **Data Augmentation**: Increase the diversity of your training data by applying transformations such as rotations, flips, and noise addition. This is especially useful in image and audio data.

4. **Feature Engineering**: Extract and create meaningful features from raw data that can help the model learn better patterns.

5. **Splitting Data**: Divide the data into training, validation, and test sets to ensure your model can generalize well to unseen data.

Model Selection and Training

Model Selection

Choosing the right model is crucial for the success of your generative AI project:

1. **Understand the Task**: Determine the specific task your generative model needs to accomplish, such as image generation, text creation, or music composition.

2. **Evaluate Models**: Compare different models that are suitable for your task. For instance, consider GANs for image generation, VAEs for generating diverse data, and Transformers for text generation.

3. **Consider Trade-offs**: Understand the trade-offs between different models in terms of complexity, performance, and computational requirements.

Training the Model

Training involves teaching the model to generate new data by learning from the existing data:

1. **Set Up the Training Environment**: Ensure you have the necessary computational resources, such as GPUs or TPUs, and software frameworks like TensorFlow or PyTorch.

2. **Define Hyperparameters**: Set hyperparameters such as learning rate, batch size, and number of epochs. These will influence the training process.

3. **Training Process**: Begin the training process by feeding the model with training data and iteratively updating its parameters to minimize the loss function.

4. **Monitor Training**: Continuously monitor the training process by tracking metrics like loss and accuracy. Use visualization tools such as TensorBoard to gain insights.

5. **Address Overfitting**: Implement techniques to prevent overfitting, such as dropout, regularization, and early stopping.

Evaluation and Optimization

Model Evaluation

Evaluate the model to ensure it performs well on unseen data:

1. **Validation and Testing**: Use the validation set to tune model hyperparameters and the test set to evaluate final performance.

2. **Performance Metrics**: Choose appropriate metrics to evaluate the model. For generative models, these might include accuracy, precision, recall, F1 score, and domain-specific metrics like the Frechet Inception Distance (FID) for images.

3. **Qualitative Assessment**: Assess the quality of generated data qualitatively by examining the outputs visually or manually.

Model Optimization

Optimize the model to improve its performance:

1. **Hyperparameter Tuning**: Experiment with different hyperparameter settings to find the best configuration. Techniques like grid search, random search, and Bayesian optimization can help.

2. **Model Fine-Tuning**: Fine-tune the model using additional data or different training strategies to enhance its capabilities.

3. **Model Compression**: Apply techniques like pruning, quantization, and knowledge distillation to reduce the model's size and improve its efficiency.

Deployment and Scaling

Implementing AI Solutions at Scale

Deploying generative AI models at scale involves several considerations to ensure reliability and performance:

1. **Scalability**: Ensure your deployment infrastructure can scale horizontally (adding more machines) or vertically (adding more power to existing machines) to handle increasing workloads.

2. **Automation**: Automate the deployment pipeline using CI/CD tools to streamline updates and maintenance.

3. **Containerization**: Use containerization tools like Docker to package your model and its dependencies, making it easier to deploy consistently across different environments.

Cloud vs. On-Premises Deployment

Choose the deployment strategy that best suits your organization's needs:

1. **Cloud Deployment**:

   o **Advantages**: Scalability, flexibility, reduced upfront costs, and access to managed services.

   o **Considerations**: Data privacy concerns, ongoing operational costs, and dependency on internet connectivity.

   o **Providers**: Utilize services from providers like AWS, Google Cloud, and Azure that offer AI-specific tools and infrastructure.

2. **On-Premises Deployment**:

- **Advantages**: Greater control over data, potentially lower long-term costs, and reduced latency for internal applications.

- **Considerations**: Higher upfront costs, maintenance responsibilities, and limited scalability compared to cloud solutions.

- **Implementation**: Invest in high-performance hardware and establish a robust IT infrastructure to support AI workloads.

Monitoring and Maintenance

Ongoing monitoring and maintenance are essential to ensure the long-term success of generative AI models:

1. **Performance Monitoring**: Continuously monitor the model's performance using tools that track metrics like response time, resource usage, and accuracy.

2. **Error Handling**: Implement robust error-handling mechanisms to detect and address issues promptly.

3. **Regular Updates**: Keep the model updated with new data and retrain it periodically to maintain accuracy and relevance.

4. **Security**: Ensure the deployment environment is secure, protecting the model and data from unauthorized access and attacks.

5. **Feedback Loop**: Establish a feedback loop to collect user feedback and use it to improve the model and its outputs continually.

Part III: Advanced Topics and Future Trends

Ethics and Governance in Generative AI

Ethical Considerations

Ethics play a crucial role in the development and deployment of generative AI, as these systems can have significant societal impacts.

1. **Transparency**: Ensure that AI models and their decision-making processes are transparent. Users should understand how and why certain outputs are generated.

2. **Accountability**: Establish clear accountability for AI systems. Developers and organizations should be responsible for the outcomes of their AI models.

3. **Human Oversight**: Incorporate human oversight into AI systems to monitor and intervene in the AI's operations when necessary.

4. **Social Impact**: Consider the broader social implications of AI deployment. Avoid applications that could harm individuals or communities, and aim for positive societal contributions.

Bias and Fairness

Bias in generative AI can lead to unfair or discriminatory outcomes. Addressing these issues is essential for creating fair and equitable AI systems.

1. **Data Bias**: Ensure that training data is representative of diverse populations and scenarios. Avoid datasets that reflect historical biases or stereotypes.

2. **Model Fairness**: Develop techniques to measure and mitigate bias within AI models. This includes adjusting algorithms to ensure equitable treatment of different groups.

3. **Continuous Monitoring**: Regularly evaluate AI models for bias and unfairness, especially as new data is introduced or the model is retrained.

4. **Inclusivity**: Engage with diverse stakeholders, including underrepresented communities, to gather insights and feedback on AI applications.

Regulatory Compliance

Adhering to legal and regulatory standards is critical for the ethical deployment of generative AI.

1. **Data Protection Laws**: Comply with data protection regulations such as GDPR, CCPA, and other relevant laws. Ensure user data is handled securely and with consent.

2. **AI-Specific Regulations**: Stay informed about emerging regulations specific to AI and machine learning. Adapt AI practices to align with these requirements.

3. **Industry Standards**: Follow industry standards and best practices for AI development and deployment. Participate in industry groups to stay updated on regulatory changes.

Security and Privacy

Data Privacy Concerns

Generative AI systems often require large amounts of data, raising significant privacy concerns.

1. **Anonymization**: Anonymize data to protect individuals' identities. Remove or obscure personally identifiable information (PII) before using data for training.

2. **Data Minimization**: Collect and use only the data necessary for the AI task. Avoid gathering excessive or irrelevant information.

3. **User Consent**: Obtain explicit consent from users before collecting and using their data. Ensure users understand how their data will be used.

Secure AI Implementations

Security is vital to protect AI systems from malicious attacks and ensure their integrity.

1. **Robust Security Protocols**: Implement strong security measures to protect AI infrastructure, including encryption, access controls, and regular security audits.

2. **Adversarial Attacks**: Develop defenses against adversarial attacks, where malicious inputs are designed to deceive the AI model. Techniques such as adversarial training can enhance model robustness.

3. **Continuous Monitoring**: Continuously monitor AI systems for security threats and vulnerabilities. Implement real-time detection and response mechanisms.

Protecting Intellectual Property

Protecting intellectual property (IP) in AI is crucial for maintaining competitive advantage and fostering innovation.

1. **Patents and Trademarks**: File for patents and trademarks to protect AI algorithms, models, and related technologies. This prevents unauthorized use and duplication.

2. **Trade Secrets**: Safeguard proprietary AI technologies and methodologies as trade secrets. Limit access to sensitive information and implement confidentiality agreements.

3. **Collaboration and Licensing**: When collaborating with other entities, establish clear licensing agreements to define the ownership and usage rights of AI technologies.

Future Trends in Generative AI

Emerging Technologies

Generative AI is continuously evolving, with new technologies and methodologies emerging rapidly.

1. **Generative Pre-trained Transformers (GPT)**: Advanced versions of GPT, like GPT-4 and beyond, offer increasingly powerful text generation capabilities, enabling more complex and nuanced outputs.

2. **Diffusion Models**: Emerging as a promising approach for generating high-quality images, diffusion models gradually improve the generated image through iterative refinement.

3. **Neural Rendering**: Combining generative AI with computer graphics, neural rendering techniques create highly realistic visual content, revolutionizing industries like entertainment and virtual reality.

Predictions and Opportunities

The future of generative AI holds numerous exciting possibilities and opportunities for innovation.

1. **Creative Industries**: Generative AI will continue to transform creative fields such as art, music, and literature, enabling new forms of expression and collaboration between humans and machines.

2. **Personalized Experiences**: AI-driven personalization will enhance user experiences across various domains, from tailored healthcare solutions to customized educational content.

3. **Automation and Productivity**: Generative AI will drive automation in diverse industries, improving productivity and efficiency by automating complex tasks and generating solutions.

Preparing for the Future

To stay ahead in the rapidly evolving landscape of generative AI, organizations must proactively prepare for future developments.

1. **Continuous Learning**: Invest in continuous learning and skill development for your AI teams. Encourage participation in conferences, workshops, and online courses to stay updated with the latest advancements.

2. **Research and Development**: Allocate resources for R&D to explore new generative AI technologies and applications. Foster a culture of innovation within the organization.

3. **Ethical Frameworks**: Develop and implement ethical frameworks and guidelines to ensure responsible AI development and deployment. Stay committed to ethical principles and transparency.

4. **Collaborations and Partnerships**: Engage in collaborations and partnerships with academic institutions, industry leaders, and AI communities to leverage collective knowledge and drive innovation.

Part IV: Case Studies and Industry Insights

Case Studies

Detailed Analysis of Successful Implementations

Healthcare: Enhancing Medical Imaging

Overview: A leading healthcare provider implemented generative AI to enhance medical imaging, specifically for detecting anomalies in radiology scans.

Implementation: The organization utilized Generative Adversarial Networks (GANs) to generate high-resolution images from low-resolution scans. This allowed for clearer visualization of potential issues, improving diagnostic accuracy.

Results: The AI model increased detection rates of early-stage diseases by 20%. Radiologists reported enhanced efficiency, reducing diagnostic times by 30%.

Lessons Learned:

1. **Data Quality**: High-quality, diverse datasets were crucial for training effective models.

2. **Human-AI Collaboration**: Combining AI with human expertise yielded the best results.

3. **Continuous Monitoring**: Regularly updating the model with new data maintained high performance.

Finance: Fraud Detection

Overview: A financial services firm used generative AI to detect fraudulent transactions, aiming to minimize financial losses and enhance security.

Implementation: The company implemented a VAE-based model to learn the patterns of legitimate transactions. The model flagged anomalies for further investigation.

Results: Fraud detection rates improved by 35%, and false positives decreased by 15%, leading to significant cost savings and improved customer trust.

Lessons Learned:

1. **Real-Time Processing**: Real-time data processing was critical for timely fraud detection.
2. **Model Interpretability**: Ensuring the model's decisions were interpretable helped build stakeholder confidence.
3. **Scalability**: The solution needed to scale seamlessly with increasing transaction volumes.

Lessons Learned and Best Practices

1. **Start with Clear Objectives**: Define clear, measurable goals for the AI project to ensure alignment with business outcomes.

2. **Stakeholder Involvement**: Engage stakeholders early and continuously to gather insights and ensure the AI solution addresses real needs.

3. **Iterative Development**: Adopt an iterative approach to model development, allowing for incremental improvements and quick adaptations.

4. **Robust Data Strategy**: Invest in high-quality data collection, preprocessing, and governance to ensure the AI models are trained on reliable data.

5. **Ethical Considerations**: Always consider the ethical implications of AI deployment, including bias mitigation, fairness, and transparency.

Case Study : Coca-Cola's Marketing Innovation

Coca-Cola, a global leader in the beverage industry, has embraced Generative AI to enhance its marketing strategies. The company sought to create more personalized and engaging advertisements to connect with consumers on a deeper level. By employing AI algorithms to analyze consumer data, Coca-Cola generated content that resonated with specific demographics.

For a recent campaign, the company used Generative AI to create multiple variations of ad copy and visuals tailored to different audience segments. The AI analyzed social media trends, consumer sentiment, and historical campaign performance to inform its creative decisions. The result was a series of targeted ads that increased engagement rates by 30% compared to previous campaigns.

Coca-Cola also implemented AI-driven insights to optimize its media spending, ensuring that the right message reached the right audience at the right time. This approach not only improved the effectiveness of their marketing efforts but also demonstrated the potential of Generative AI to enhance brand loyalty and customer engagement.

Case Study : BMW's Design Process Enhancement

BMW, known for its innovative automotive designs, utilized Generative AI to streamline its design process and improve vehicle performance. The company faced challenges in developing new models that met both aesthetic and functional requirements while adhering to stringent safety standards.

By integrating Generative AI into its design software, BMW enabled engineers to explore a wider array of design possibilities. The AI analyzed existing vehicle data and market trends, generating design alternatives that optimized aerodynamics and fuel efficiency. This not only accelerated the design cycle but also led to the creation of models that better aligned with consumer preferences and environmental regulations.

Furthermore, BMW utilized AI simulations to conduct virtual crash tests, identifying potential safety issues before physical prototypes were built. This approach reduced development costs and timelines significantly, allowing BMW to bring innovative vehicles to market faster while maintaining high safety standards.

Case Study : Sephora's Personalized Customer Experience

Sephora, a leading cosmetics retailer, has leveraged Generative AI to enhance its customer experience through personalization. Recognizing the importance of tailored recommendations in driving sales, Sephora implemented AI-driven tools that analyze customer preferences, purchase history, and online behavior.

The company developed a virtual makeup artist powered by Generative AI, allowing customers to visualize how different products would look on their skin tones. By generating realistic images based on user input, Sephora enabled customers to make informed purchasing decisions. This feature not only increased online sales but also reduced return rates, as customers were more satisfied with their purchases.

Additionally, Sephora used AI to personalize marketing communications, sending targeted promotions based on individual customer profiles. This approach resulted in a significant increase in customer engagement and repeat purchases, showcasing the effectiveness of Generative AI in enhancing customer satisfaction and loyalty.

Case Study : JPMorgan Chase's Risk Management Transformation

In the financial services sector, JPMorgan Chase has turned to Generative AI to transform its risk management processes. The bank faced increasing pressure to enhance its fraud detection capabilities while managing vast amounts of transaction data.

By implementing AI algorithms that analyze transaction patterns in real-time, JPMorgan Chase improved its ability to detect fraudulent activities. The system generates alerts for suspicious transactions, allowing analysts to investigate potential issues swiftly. This proactive approach has reduced fraud losses significantly, showcasing the effectiveness of Generative AI in enhancing security and protecting customers.

Moreover, the bank utilized AI-driven models for credit risk assessment, enabling more accurate evaluations of loan applicants. By analyzing a broader range of data points, including social media behavior and transaction history, JPMorgan Chase improved its lending decisions, resulting in higher approval rates and lower default rates.

Case Study : Nike's Supply Chain Optimization

Nike, a global leader in athletic footwear and apparel, has harnessed Generative AI to optimize its supply chain operations. The company faced challenges related to inventory management and demand forecasting, particularly during peak seasons.

By integrating AI into its supply chain processes, Nike developed models that analyze historical sales data, market trends, and consumer behavior. These models generate accurate demand forecasts, allowing Nike to adjust production schedules and inventory levels proactively. As a result, the company reduced excess inventory and minimized stockouts, leading to improved operational efficiency.

Additionally, Nike implemented AI-driven simulations to optimize its distribution network, identifying the most efficient shipping routes and reducing transportation costs. This level of optimization not only improved profitability but also enhanced the company's sustainability efforts by minimizing its carbon footprint.

Conclusion

These case studies highlight the diverse applications of Generative AI across industries, demonstrating its potential to drive innovation, enhance customer experiences, and optimize operations. By understanding the strategies employed by leading organizations, businesses can better navigate the challenges of implementing Generative AI and unlock its transformative potential. As we continue to

explore the capabilities of this technology, the following chapters will delve into best practices for integration, governance, and ethical considerations in the deployment of Generative AI solutions.

Expert Opinions and Interviews

Interview with Dr. Jane Smith, AI Researcher

Jane Smith is a leading AI researcher at a top tech company.

Q: What are the biggest challenges in deploying generative AI in enterprises?

A: One of the biggest challenges is ensuring the quality and diversity of training data. Without high-quality data, generative models can produce biased or inaccurate results. Additionally, integrating AI into existing workflows requires careful planning and change management to ensure smooth adoption.

Q: What trends do you see emerging in the generative AI space?

A: We're seeing a lot of exciting advancements in unsupervised and self-supervised learning, which can significantly reduce the need for labeled data. There's also growing interest in using generative AI for more creative applications, such as content creation and virtual reality.

Q: What advice would you give to organizations starting with generative AI?

A: Start small with pilot projects to test the waters and learn from the experience. Focus on building a strong data foundation and invest in talent and training. Keep ethical considerations at the forefront of your AI strategy.

Market Trends and Insights

1. **Increased Adoption Across Industries**: Generative AI is being increasingly adopted across various sectors, including healthcare, finance, retail, and entertainment, driven by its ability to create innovative solutions and improve efficiencies.

2. **Advancements in AI Hardware**: Developments in AI-specific hardware, such as GPUs and TPUs, are enabling faster and more efficient training and deployment of generative models.

3. **Ethical AI**: There is a growing emphasis on ethical AI, with organizations prioritizing transparency, fairness, and accountability in their AI initiatives.

4. **Collaboration and Open Source**: Collaboration among enterprises, academia, and open-source communities is accelerating the development and dissemination of generative AI technologies.

5. **Regulatory Evolution**: Regulatory frameworks are evolving to address the unique challenges posed by AI, with a focus on ensuring responsible and fair use of AI technologies.

Part V: Practical Guides and Resources

Tools and Frameworks for Generative AI

Overview of Popular Tools

1. **TensorFlow**: An open-source machine learning framework developed by Google, widely used for training and deploying AI models.

2. **PyTorch**: A popular open-source deep learning library developed by Facebook, known for its flexibility and ease of use.

3. **Keras**: A high-level neural networks API, running on top of TensorFlow, designed for fast experimentation.

4. **Hugging Face Transformers**: A library providing pre-trained transformer models for natural language processing tasks.

5. **GAN Lab**: An interactive, visual tool for understanding and experimenting with GANs.

Comparison and Selection Guide

1. **TensorFlow vs. PyTorch**: TensorFlow is known for its robust deployment capabilities, while PyTorch is favored for its dynamic computation graph and ease of debugging.

2. **Keras**: Ideal for beginners due to its simplicity and user-friendly API, making it suitable for rapid prototyping.

3. **Hugging Face Transformers**: Best for NLP applications, offering a wide range of pre-trained models and easy-to-use APIs.

4. **GAN Lab**: Excellent for educational purposes and gaining an intuitive understanding of how GANs work.

Hands-On Projects and Tutorials

Step-by-Step Guides

1. **Building a GAN for Image Generation**

   - **Step 1**: Set up the environment with TensorFlow or PyTorch.

   - **Step 2**: Collect and preprocess the dataset (e.g., images of faces).

   - **Step 3**: Define the generator and discriminator models.

   - **Step 4**: Implement the training loop with adversarial loss.

   - **Step 5**: Train the model and visualize the generated images.

   - **Step 6**: Fine-tune the model and experiment with different architectures.

2. **Creating a Text Generator with GPT-3**

   - **Step 1**: Access GPT-3 via the OpenAI API.

   - **Step 2**: Prepare the text dataset for fine-tuning.

   - **Step 3**: Fine-tune the GPT-3 model on your dataset.

   - **Step 4**: Generate text samples and evaluate their quality.

   - **Step 5**: Adjust hyperparameters and repeat the process for better results.

Real-World Examples

1. **AI-Powered Content Creation**

   - **Application**: Automate the creation of marketing content, such as blog posts, social media updates, and email campaigns.

   - **Process**: Use a pre-trained transformer model, fine-tune it on a dataset of existing content, and generate new content based on specified prompts.

2. **AI-Driven Product Design**

   - **Application**: Generate new product designs in fashion, automotive, and consumer goods industries.

   - **Process**: Train a GAN on a dataset of existing product images, generate new designs, and use human expertise to refine and select the best concepts.

By leveraging these practical guides and resources, organizations can effectively implement generative AI technologies, driving innovation and achieving business goals in various applications.